OTHERHOOD

PITT POETRY SERIES

Ed Ochester, Editor

OTHERHOOD

poems

Reginald Shepherd

UNIVERSITY OF PITTSBURGH PRESS

The publication of this book is supported by a grant
from the Pennsylvania Council on the Arts.

Published by the University of Pittsburgh Press, Pittsburgh, Pa., 15260
Copyright © 2003, Reginald Shepherd
Manufactured in the United States of America
Printed on acid-free paper
10 9 8 7 6 5 4 3 2 1
ISBN 0-8229-5797-3

FOR ROBERT PHILEN

Contents

IV

I

Reasons for Living

We're walking with the backwards
river, sluggish water dialects
spell out spilled lakefront's
tumbledown babble of dressed
stones, nervous dogs and "no
swimming" pictographs: the land
washes ashore with under
clinging to it, undermining
crumble, halted fall. We pick our way
to level rock, watch out for oblique
angle slabs, it's so hot
we take off our pants, we lie down
and are grass, that green
and spore-filled, well-adapted
to be carried on the wind.

Mold-colored water dulled
by use (pastel, muddled
nephrite, more common
than true jade, less highly prized,
its luster oily rather than vitreous,
a scum spilled across perspective)
with a turquoise line to build horizon
out of: prehnite, andradite,
alkali tourmaline, a seam of
semiprecious chrysoprase: anything
but true emerald, a grass-green beryl,
smaragdos, prized for medicinal
virtues: uvarovite even rarer
among garnets, its crystals typically
too small to cut.

A broken landscape (man-made)
says to its place, "I don't
remember you," unphrased,
grooved by the gaze, chiseled
into being unseen, a glancing
blow: incursions of the geometric
(cement no place to rest your head),
naked economy, awkward skin
on green towels. And then a stirring
at the other side of when,
complicit blood flows back
into the stem, in retrospect
unfinished: we stand up
erect as grass, xylem, parenchyma,
epidermis, leaf blade and sheath.

An Abbreviated History of Signs

And not to be removed
under penalty of law, the lovers
meditating on conjunction, *for*,

with, *among* not touching, sounds
that cleave them, seam them, each I seen
to be an eye. This *and* comes

between them, baffles in a labyrinth
of vowel songs (*I owe you*): longs
not to be a part of speech

apart. While they say *world*, things
go on adding up promiscuously,
repeating *brick, yellow, drink*: every

fish, finch, swallow, apparent
young man; window panes
glance, blink, and blur. (Light lies

like a dog across the threshold, willing
to find gods in anything, Daphne
boughs, bones of the tree.) Seeds

stiffen into branches, rooted leaves
sprout stems, sewing damp ground
to sky, the pure devouring light

of hands: no sound missing
in the wind, loose coins of leaves
(fernlike, much dissected, orange

-red to purple) lacunae shaken
from dripping limbs, scarlet
sumac dropping: *like* flies

out and under: rumbles, rustles.
(He loved the liquid consonants'
consequence, consanguinity

glossed across wet sidewalks
said before. Here's a theory
of the small of his back, spine's

scooped-out channel run aground
on shallow breathing.) *To* and *two*
make *thou*, loss feeds on light

(sciosophy, the science of shadows,
burning the wish to be seen),
according with the lapses

in the law. Days pass
through his body as though
he were glass, *I* seems

a ceremony of sums, adds
an absence to the eye: dangles
there upside down. Argued

into experience, cutting days
down to sight, the origins
of space in ruined shine.

Kingdom: An Epithalamium

Who is it that cometh up from
a spring shut, a fountain sealed,
terrible as an army with banners

(*Your name*, or 'you')

Sought him, but found him not,
because the sun hath looked upon me
with one chain of his neck

(*Voice*, or sound of his approach)

I will go up to the palm tree
which hath a most vehement flame;
every man hath his sword upon his thigh

(These were the mountain dwellings)

Draw me, we will run after thee
until the day break shadows
If he be a wall, we will build upon him

(as they lie together in the open air)

My head is filled with dew
and those that keep the fruit thereof
upon the handles of the lock

(*Winter*, the rainy season)

Who is this that cometh out
like pillars of smoke. If he be a door
I am a wall, and like towers

Little Hands

Here actors estrange themselves
from acts. Glare ladles light
across the radius, high canopies
luxuriant with epiphytes, trees
are shaken into green, drench
of wind disturbing leaves
to drunken semaphores: little
hands designing new catamites
for outmoded gods.

2

At this time every year
divinity died, the Adonis
flowed red with his blood:
clay runoff from the Lebanon.

3

Chipped singing of arrowheads
and off-white statuary scree
plowed up in a burnt west field
declining a little into afternoon
(some columns broken off
mid-thought) rings against
well-rusted blades: a waste
of monuments, miles of ravens
and manure, rivers
with the names of trees,
the Cedar flooding summer.

Rome's staple crop
was wheat—called corn—along
with barley, raised for stock
feed and some places
for beer: peas and beans
also, though forbidden
by Pythagoras. The slow
-maturing olive; figs, pome
-granates, plums; grapevines
trained on a variety of trees.

4

The man becomes a boy eventually
(blank body a white page
where wishes write themselves): shape
left behind by the sculpture wind,
but stamped with it nonetheless. Certain
human behaviors propagate gods,
nostalgia for the whole he's been
referred to: an exercise of will
around the block, through the park
and down the hill, the possibilities
still unexhausted. Some are games
and some have numbers, some
are hollow, make a ringing sound.

5

Silence, item, silence.

6

The god fucks himself with a fig branch
above the open grave, admirer
of hopeless machines—starling

pasted to the street, dysfunctional
flying contraption; the god
forsakes himself for his own sake
(pledged to slick feathers
frescoed on funerary pavement),
takes himself back to him. *Whore,*
they honor him in caves
and tearoom stalls, alleys
and temple courtyards. Color
is light's continuity, the stem
still new to the trunk, leaf
darkening to fruit, to seeds.

7

Mere world, where every man's
the artist of himself, body
his medium, interference (an inference
at most). The statues sweating, overflowing
with the fear of form, prefabricated
weather on the other side of glass:
cute guys in various states of disrepair
sighted from across the burning bridge,
and voices in salt water singing
"pale Gomorrah." I walked into my ocean,
meet me under the whale.

Flicker

scatters afternoon across blank
water, warmest by late September,
an artifice of lakefront's
drowning weather. Scuba

divers strip off black flippers,
no bodies recovered today. The
secretive shore moves stealthily
up to and exceeding its limits,

green wave crests higher than
concrete banks, barrier dunes'
collected complaints against
wave and sand's copulation,

contamination of divide.
Horizoned to a skein of sheen
and weatherblown smooth, lake
asymptote is interrupted by intervals

of pumping platforms: small islands
in the mind, moments of thing
and motion, less. Shapes
movement leaves behind

in the eye, imagoes of its afterward:
herring gull hung against sun setting
on the other side, west match
set to oiled water, but at a distance

watching knows. (A film reflecting
vaguely on a wavering world
of absences and outlines, anecdotal
figures blurring into view.) Leaves

waiting for burning already take
burnt colors, huddled on highway
trees, red lights, squabble of gulls
settles on wet bread crumbs, skittish

sand: an accident in progress
at twenty-four frames a second
holds still, distills spilled light
to artifacts in the floating eye

marrying empty space to sky.

For Gabrielle Karras

The Invention of Longitude

Unsolved: frost clotting a broken
tree, a clutch of feathers giving up
a thing hooked on a branch. Image
wrack of silver-leafed plants taken

to be snow, something driven by the sea
of words for winter wind, when winter's
not yet here: *Artemisia stellarana*,
Senecio maritimus. A box of curiosity

the cold unfolds, *Stella Maris*, steering
by angular displacement, an ephemeris
of the moon for every noon and midnight.
(Radius of heading, bearing down, point of arrival

departing for perspective dwindling
to pipe-stemmed rain, the sifting mist
horizon recedes from place.) Rust-red
September ends here, stains wet pavements

as if summer forgot itself, sprawled out and bled
to death: an early iteration, wholly lacking
the capacity for flight. Blue signposts, news
reports and labels, events of evergreens

tracking and measuring storms. Star
-fish, starfoot, death by synecdoche
and star-shaped leaves: sky fallen through
part of a hole, all douse by now. I heard

you spoke once, flowerboat,
the bone casing breathed like an idea
stepping inside the body of a bird
who has approached too close to motion.

Wing under Construction

Ophiussa, mother of snakes
where he resides with too much
resemblance, boy branching into coral

storm-washed icon (island
lions almost gone by now), several
species of acacia, lowland pine

Slim hipped, 'the black-haired folk'

Alasiya, Yadnana, Kipros, Kubris
'the word for copper in modern
European languages, but not in Greek'

2

Fish-bellied Derceto turns men into carp
and feeds them to piecemeal virgins:
they sink through the slur
of salt until the loss floats home
like jetsam
     White bull dies on
the beach and she
bathes naked in black blood, chaste
paradise where all is possible
and nothing is forgiven: paradise

chased into black mud, shoots
up like deep-rooted marram grass
holding the hills in place

3

No teeth draw blood like his kiss,
dictum, dialect, 'though we cannot
date it or identify its origin'

Little bottle of him stoppered up,
piss water, lymph, semen wash
sealed in a copper flask

4

Day splits like lightning,
copper rain, and love
rides in on the ninth wave (stiff
-beaten waves start over, chips of
blue snow, open vowels, cypress bark):

5

steps from the Phoenician
half shell with chaos
for wake (spume of
red corpuscles, spilled sperm)

medicinal kelp burning
in bitter hand, salve for
sky's scythed-off genitals

6

Zostera marina, ruined
shrine of drying eelgrass
cured on sharp rocks

Faience figurine fragment
inlaid with gold, imported ivory
probably Eros

7

All love is unrequited, unrequired
(carnage of scattered sand
dollars), I built a bight or cove of him

In the City of Elagabal

the victorious sun will kill us
at noon, fatal light loves us

'The firstborn of thy sons
shalt thou likewise
give to me': burned bones
buried in urns under stelae

≈

'His idol taken from a town in Egypt
also called Heliopolis': a sacrificial altar
with its fire always lit

≈

'a priest will come, the last of all,
sent from the sun, and he will do everything
by craft; the city of the sun
will arise': based mainly
on the votive inscriptions of the tophet

≈

Ugarit Baalbek Byblos ablaze

it's been said

≈

The sun never dies. The sun descends
into the netherworld, battles
the demons of the night sea,
is in danger, but does not die.

dies natales solis invicti

they found him as handsome
as a Phoenician prince

'We know the rest of the story'

when summer came, he went down
into earth's bowels, the fruit trees
were abandoned to terrible heat

the personal part of his theonymic
(Hammon: HMN) continues to raise problems

'*Ela*, a god, and *Gabal*, to form, the forming
or plastic god; a proper, and even happy
epithet': which could refer
to the fire of the sun
or the fire of the sacrifices
ambivalently

sheer light: unscalable, indefensible
but with a certain distance
from itself: 'the *dominus caeli*
of Saint Augustine, who knew of
his existence'

the child became a hero after its passage through fire

so it has been suggested that Baal Hammon
may be lord of the perfume altars

⌒

the fire is not stoked but fanned
to ensure complete combustion;
when calcination is sufficient
a handful of sand extinguishes it

in the summer, the young god died

⌒

as if the sun were lost, carried off

'When thou returnest, we will greet thee
as a friend.'

⌒

'under the form of a black conical stone'
'which had fallen from heaven on that most sacred'

this too is labeled: 'LH'GBL
which was the god's presence

⌒

Seleucia Antioch Emesa
a single flame

⌒

and Herakles, whose deeds also included
mounting a funeral pyre
with an eagle duly perched upon it

(to these objects a lamp is added)

⌒

'his personal interests melted away
in the fire of the feverish search'
concerned to make the offering on high

✎

the firstborn child belonged to Baal

'To begin with the pious had wanted to count them
to see whether the number corresponded
to the days of the solar year.'

but it would probably be wrong to reduce all these
to a single common denominator

✎

this nomad tribe worshipped a faceless
formless fire spirit

(the sun is danger, irremediable)

'The richest wines, the most extraordinary victims,
and the rarest aromatics, were profusely consumed
on his altar.'

(habitual calamity of light)

✎

a stone baked by the daytime sun
preserves a little of its heat at night,
as if the sun remained in it

✎

Laodicea 'the Burnt', so called
from the furnaces of the quicksilver mines
at Zizima

✎

which is like agitated water on which light is flashing
(which is like agitated light

in flashing water)

a luxury of flame, I am beside myself
with burning, a hecatomb
of parch and wither

'with the fire she scorched him, so that his fate
was fulfilled'

Non omnis moriar.

⚬

nicknamed Heliogabalus, equivalent of an insult like
'scoundrel of the Sun'

⚬

burning a lamb instead of a child, like Abraham
in the arms of a bronze statue of Kronos (Baal
Hammon of the Carthaginians, Saturn
of Roman Africa)

⚬

'Thy name is He-Who-Expels, oh, He-Who-Expels!'
who could only be perceived in fire and an inner voice

(it is useless to add that no archaeological
document has provided the slightest)

⚬

the sun conceived of as a warlike blazing
the birthday of the invincible

⚬

'And he caused his children
to pass through the fire'

thousands of such urns have been found

hmm* : 'hot' or 'burning,' already
mentioned

the god could well be lord of the furnaces
'which they have built in the high places of Tophet'

although coming down to us in poorer condition
because they had been at least partly subjected
to the cremation fires: a hand holding the lightning,
or by a foot

puissant Baal is dead
long life to puissant Baal

(he is nothing, he is grit against
the palm, where the tallow
turns to brown)

it used to be I'd lie with dust

even if it may allude in passing to the fire

'What we would like to know more about are the temples
in which these priests officiated':
perhaps a sprig of cypress, a tree
consecrated to the Sun

the meaning would be 'God Mountain'

II

Periplus

The way the lake is a fact, yes: cold water
is on fire, flames
fleck off on the palm, pour out (gold sands
of the River Pactolus, King Sun
metals afternoon, gilds fingers
stiff): an occasion of light and movement
in the phenomenal world.

Knife edge of fact, contrast
so keen it draws blood: sand and fresh
water, jetty and waves subsiding
as one: a sharp pebble or glass
shard cuts bare dirty feet, infects
the body with late September.
You see that a fact
has a form, feel its imprint for weeks.

1. visible only in the event of
2. pieced into broken soil and pebbles
3. sifting the preceding absences
4. when the sun is precisely at meridian
5. oil slick in a clogged sewer grate
6. hitting tumbledown stones at such an angle
7. water not burning because already burned
8. barring any similar seasonal occurrence
9. fire, or other process of oxidization
10. _____

Mare Tyrrhenum
Mare Adriaticum

Mare Aegaeum
Pontus Euxinus
Mare Hyrcanium

    🖋

Drawbridge rising over the redirected
Chicago River to let two barges
under (rusted machinery
of motion, lift and heave):
the river a massive purchase
on time, slow gallons going in reverse.

    🖋

Things go down the North Branch
and get dirty, new words
I've no resistance to, *welter*
and *gully*, *runnel* and *mulch*,
foaming at the aeration pipes.

    🖋

Mare Mediterraneum
"the sea between the lands"

monsters here (whirlpools
as well, clashing rocks)

    🖋

Still life, still life, rows of
heaped-up dead things: starling
merging with mud and decaying weeds
by the park pond, clouds filigreed with
reflective poisons (the start
of water), a drawbridge broken over
Cermak Avenue. Monarch
glued to the broad way, one wing

perpendicular to street (orange
and black sail, flag of
convenience), one black
-furred body spilled on asphalt.

This bird that claims the morning
branch and makes the tree a factory
of song. Song scars cold air.

Blue One Lake

The river whispers *boys are boys,*
this is a glass of dust, and he
drinks slowly (this is the grass), as in

anticipation. He knows before the day
is over day will leave, thinks his hands
are made of glass, refract

and dissect ardors coolly lit, sharp edges
cut and cutting. (And in the corner
a man's peddling rain: *into, away*

from, he croons, but I don't want
any more.) Eros slides down the blue
hill (an appetite in place of self), next

sky overclouded, and crammed with
substitutions. (When I use him up
there will be more.) This is the hand

that wounds, his armature
of grace (armor, dishonor
me) brushes against black fur

-whales and forgets to drown: certain
as water, grammar of grace and fall
and comes before *and*. He's put to work

on the thunder, a surfeit of surfaces
and untethered oceans. (Little box
of what he is, splurge-weed and bottle

-wrack.) Season of smudged smoke, a
something, beautiful remains:
next time he is the snow.

Burnt from the Notebooks

His boyhood loves him, clings
to his skin: pungent smell of lemons,
crushed mint and eucalyptus leaves
heal air, laurel twins verdant hair:

thinks he is myrtle, evergreen
of marriage, mourning too, carves
him out of myth and solitary
white flowers, black fruit

Clove, allspice, evening primrose
where evening never calls:
he relies entirely on absence
republic of volatile oils

clearing an empty place in the mind
repeating each punctual gesture
(taking his place in the empty mind
small island of climbing vines)

The god is a boy whose arrows
have been stolen, snapped
one by one by my humiliated hands

useful for kindling now

Sunday blush of boys cruising
crackling leaves and trash, faith in
redundancy's ruthless youth

(out looking for just a piece
of sex, torn phallic branchlet
oozing camphor, eugenol)

contingencies of shedding trees
and buildings under demolition,
construction dust of new condominiums

(as if desire had a history, came down
with clinging vines ripped from red bricks
small thorns scoring my palms)

&

Forecast clouds fold open, let go
of their resentments: rain
strips October bare

Syntax

Occasionally a god speaks to you,
rutted tollway a flint knife breaching
gutted fields hung on event

horizon, clear cut contradiction
through soybeans and sheared corn: blue
pickup an orange blaze, white letters

blistered, boiling down to tarmac,
asphalt, sulfur fume cured by a methane
gas burn-off pipe, blue flame chipped

with white raising a buttress of weather
-burnt bricks, flaking wind
totem. We stopped to take some cargo

on, weighted October with a freight
of waiting snow traveling east, panic of
starlings startled from stubble husks

by a harvest moon dangled directly
ahead: drove into the pitted sphere, bloody
pearl punched in a sky just out of reach

(vanishing point retreating, peeling),
one of the yellowed streetlights
by now, dimming, diminishing. The road

says to perspective, *wait*.

Polaroid

1

Propositions, presuppositions,
a small summer in my palm.
It hollowed out a heart
in me, backdrop of burned leaves
and singed color. October
evening recovers summer, renders it
Oil Drum Fire with Bum huddled
at horizon, glittering past
complacency. These

2

*early lighthouses had wood fires
or torches in the open, sometimes
sheltered by a roof.* Tungsten lamps
fizz on at five to six, flaring like myth
in the making with borrowed
bits of shine. No getting around that
smooth skin, sealed envelope of poison.

3

Let empire, let rage: I said
to worms, you are my mother
and my sister (unearth my then),
we are death's firstborn
festival. The young men
saw me and hid, and the old men
smiled like ash: waited for me
as for rain, acid, for the most part
memory.

4

I cover the sea's voice with chalk
and circumstance, having only myself
to say, scattered smattering of singed
doll parts. They make their way
by means of breakings (schist
and marl): collapse into a clamor
of crows before appearances'
sake, and stand simple

5

in their wreckage. *Coal by-product*
ovens extract ammonia, tar, light oils
wasted as smoke when coal burns:

the mindless heat of substitution
tended and intended, burning
razed fields flat as photographs.

6

Pillar and halt, pillar
and stall, a sinking
water table leaves behind
its salt: the man I made of him.

Confluence

Summer held its breath
too long, green grapes grew crazy,
swelled and burst. Insects, of
course, also arachnids; centipedes,
millipedes. Misfortunes
of September finches preen
on autumn berms.
                      Hosed down sunlight
horizons destructions, hissing
from the feathered wounds
where every kindness
is punished with ravens. A gap
torn in the fabric of the city, damage
to marbled skin.
                      Anywhere
an anchor, harbor in air, things waiting
to be revised. The dead man
rises from his gravel body
tomb, green turtle pebbles shatter,
scattering. Love is this winter
rising in an acrid wind, talismans of place
(polluted lake) subjected
to presentation.
                      His only distance
will be horses, frontal herd
stampeding tides and currents
the one recorded interruptus.
Shored up with stored foam
deckle, scudding margin
kelp cures shine on stone.

Three Songs about Snow

1

I spoke every week
into weather (wheel, hub,
axle sky with turning

vapor trails, high rises). Clouds
let go of letting go, hail sleet, snow
snares light, glare ice

by midnight. Flurried sun
a hook to hang perceptions, grapple,
pulley, hauls in salted gravel.

2

I hide myself, but am
no one, come into view
the same white

overpass, cars tossed
underhand across the lane
divider, line dividing gray

-brown field and gray
-white afternoon:
I am a dark

3

Each day almost believable
adhering to protocol:

incidents of water
at an oblique angle to air

a whole ragged silk
of torn storm

I climbed his voice
when it was cold

Amant Marine

Remembered limbs as a because,
swan box of tethered monodies,
rope and pulley, winch of extinct

gods: saw me deserting my grief's
oligarchy of referential skin,
abraded by the glacier for the greater

good. A truck full of snow
and residual narrative
let the winter into him,

wore him down to spurious
fragment pressing silence, Icarus's
ocean-splayed weight, cold water

that once touched the bare leg of him.
(Gulls notch the waves he's lustered
under, hieratic sea-green chords

take off the Orpheus mask.) The teachers
of flight prepared him well
to be a broken tally of a man,

museum pigeon wholly lacking
the capacity for flight: unable
to recall unfolded wings

and down he goes, phoenix
-sided, phoenix-stride, white
throat rusted away.

Les Semblables

Stringent syntax of brick dust, cracked
leaves, broken up
pavement and a dead finch, dun
feathers dusted with brick
grit, all the same
color, mine:
         something
will be built there
I can't afford, blue sky
of your terrifying mouth,
my roof without a ceiling
leaking wind
        Adore, a door
burnt open, lintel, jamb still
standing, salvaged brick
and timber:
        "carrying the load
above an opening"

        Persistent drone
of sky, high tension wire, jet
contrail, drift of Canada
geese incised on clouds
cut off midshape, trailing
water particles
        Wingspan at meridian
turned on an anecdotal wheel,
a clutch of ruined wind

Strict noon criteria, qualifying,
qualifying, when isn't a god unlucky
for his lovers

Roman Year

Martius

The corrugated iron gates
are rolling down storefronts
in paradise, late light flecks windows,
rain's acid fingerprints. Motes
float between iron and glass, sink
into sanded pavements, weather's
footprints, cracked *mappa mundi*: silk
tea roses with a fringe of plastic fern;
grapes, apples, and bananas ripened
to painted wax: your eyes
blinking away pollen
in wind that says spring's coming, wait
for me. Months sometimes it takes

Aprilis

light scrolls across an unmade bed,
we were setting out for Aries
in paper planes (white dwarf stars
bright in a wilderness of wish scatter
white feathers among me, fistfuls
of light): bees busied themselves
with the seen, moment's
multiple tasks, for the pollen, honey
in the blood, bees would drown
each day: from a thicket of nos
to one sepaled blossoming, all
in an afternoon

you thought of bees as summer

Maius

This heliotrope gaze has fixed me
in its sights (the turning solar year suffers
in sudden rain, grazes my cold
with vague waves, plashing
particles, but lightly): lightly
take this sky, bound up in so much
loose light, light wind brushes chapped
lips. Light-footed gods break open
day to see what it contains: body
survives light's inquisitions.

Junius

Beside the shale pigeons a dove
color of old brick dust, the sound
of brick dust settling: traffic noise
rides heat-rise off wet streets, summer
music echoes borrowed air: light
centrifugal, sent scattering, lost later
every day: some gold
against bright water (handfuls
scattered over lake), unnecessary, true
candleland waning to wax
and wick, silver water shattering
like backed glass

Quintilis

When I was in Egypt, light fell
instead of rain, congealed to grains of sand,
pyramidal, uninterred. Uninterrupted waves
of palms departed for shuddering oases. Why was it
I spent centuries in that mirage, caravanserai
of the sirocco stopped, pausing at

reflection, also called the polished sky,
and still no fall of shade? The light hung
triangular, aslant, touched the colossus
to song.

Sextilis

Wanting to understand, not wanting
to understand, worried that
by taking thought you lose it, by not
taking thought. Watching him run a hand
through thin blond hair, passing
at arm's length on a lunch hour
street. Wondering *is it good now, am I
pleasure*, and *which part is it that I need*,
while air migrates too slowly to be seen
and noon crawls groggy over August
skin. Then thinking *No, it's too*
and turning back to look at traffic.

September

Sudden storm, then sudden sun. *Give me*,
I almost said: and stopped, began again
with your voice, what gets invented by the
I-can't-say-that-here. The afternoon of after rain
dazzles with cloudlessness and a painful green
set casually against blue: light
mottled by fractal leaves
freckles your outstretched arm,
repeating *apple, apple, apple*, sour
fruit and crabgrass. A damp T-shirt
takes on that color, nothing
will wash it out. I wear it for weeks.

October

doorway, flutter, moth
or leaf in flight, in fall
foyer, stammer of wind, a patter
hovering, dust hushed or
pressed to trembling
glass, smut, soot, mutter
of moth or withered stem,
late haze, gray stutter
crumpled, crushed,
falter, fall, a tread . . .

November

williwaw, brawl in air,
shunt or sinew of wind shear
blown off course, pewter skew
vicinity, winnow and complicit

sky preoccupied with grizzle,
winter feed of lawns' snared
weathervane, whey-faced day
brume all afternoon of it

(lead reticence of five o'clock)
remnant slate all paucity and drift
salt splay, slur and matte brink
snow stammers against sidewalks

December

White light seen through
the season's double window
clouding the room reveals the roses'

week-old gift of petals bruised purple-black.
Dry paper falling on white cloth
seconds the white room's wonder
at cold sun flurried, crumbling stars
compacted underfoot: lattice
of fixed clarity, wintrish eidolon
half patience, half at prayer.

III

Homology

At last the myth as
such, the murderous flesh
of him, bird wire
hum, arterial. Stars shift
into focus, out, the sun
is danger, irremediable
(*remove my burden*
and produce for me
a name): leaves its finger
-prints on everything.
Apollo is black, wolf to
the moon, *Sol* burnt
to cinders in my blind eye
(black stone sears sky, white
shadow covers day). Sun's
heat consumes moon,
but there is water
under earth. Eyes neither
blue nor green, something
between *no* and *yes*: drift
and murmured *undo*
all crumpled-paper
afternoon. A voice says
Let's stay in bed
today, a voice says
When? Eleven occurrences
of the pronoun *I*,
sound of gold and broken
pieces of machine (you and
your pocket splendors, never

mind), doors never close properly
in dreams. A funnel full of
books and the usual
damage, pornography
to concentrate the mind.
Successfully overlaying
underling (is there something
else you'd rather want?),
pent up with pen and paper
birds (blisses of ravens, murders
of crows). Doubt collects in
cluttered rain gutters, festers
with rotting moonlight, leaves
drunk on too much resemblance.
And; but; oh; then I was
in his room; no; because;
it's you again. Eros
goes shaking the bushes
for sex (saving appearances'
stake in things), men fall from
ripe branches: apples, quinces,
pomegranates, pears. In
pairs, legs intertwined
and glued with sweat. And
something almost evident
makes its way toward
intransigence, opacity
of other people's bodies.
(I move the stones
into my shadow.) Sparrow
-body (broken), sparrow
hawk summer drowns:
what will love do now?

The relation existing
between compounds in a series
whose successive members
have in composition
a regular difference.

Hygiene

> how do you like your blueeyed boy
> Mister Death
>
> *e.e. cummings*

1

Some men wash their hands five times
a day and still feel dirty. Ablutomania,
mysophobia, who can be clean
enough? *Just look at your fingernails!*
Everyone in this town's still washing his hands
of Jeffrey Dahmer, it's
1993, fifty degrees at noon
in May.
             "For a lot of black guys it's a treat
to sleep with a white man." I'm sure
there's no one who wouldn't go down on death (*your*
blueeyed boy), forget to come up
for air: I have been half in love
myself. He's dead by now, found them
at the Grand Avenue Mall, the unfashionable
Club 219, where white men sometimes go
to pick up hot black numbers (never mine).
Couldn't you just eat him up right there? Come
here. Eleven skulls, one skeleton, a freezer
stocked with body parts. They found bones
in the basement they still can't identify.
Identified with him. I found myself.

Every white man on my bus home looks
like him, what I'd want to be destroyed
by, want to be. (I thought I would

abase myself for love or any damage:
I was wrong.) The man next to me
wouldn't touch me, moved away
when I sat down. One day I'll wash my hands
of this, a waste of all that circumstance, waste of
my good time. His more than one hundred pages
of confession note "my consuming lust to experience
their bodies." Every white man
I can see. What's it like not to want? It's late
May in Milwaukee, thirty degrees at night.

2

A man naked in bed beside you has a smell
that's quite particular, not unpleasant but
distinct. It stays in the room all morning
after he's gone, you don't know where
it comes from. You'd like to know
what's in his head, or what he had
for lunch. Asleep, the body lying
next to you seems just so much
red meat, some matter muttering
to itself. Dead bodies have a smell also
which some men will do anything
to understand. Who wouldn't want
to feel what he has felt, these
clumsy hands on every interior
of him? Not I, but sometimes
always *me*, small case
against. "Mass murderers are men
who can't control their interest
in other people." They're men consumed
by curiosity. Close enough to get inside
his skin, to take his smell and make it

53

mine. They couldn't get the smell
out of the building; I can't get this
out of me. An experiment
in how to become someone else
who isn't moving anymore.

Apollo on What the Boy Gave

Eyes the color of winter water,
eyes the winter of water where I

Quoits in the Spartan month
Hyacinthius, the game
joins us, pronounces
us god and boy: I toss him
the discus thinking *This is mine*
and wind says *Not yet*

Memory with small hairs
pasted to pale wet skin
(the flower *hyacinthos*,
perhaps a fritillaria, not
the modern *Hyacinthus orientalis*)

After he smells of orange groves,
spreads white ass meat for me
him with a hole drilled in him I keep trying
to fill: I ease my way into his orchard

(the ornamental Liliaceae
genera, including the spring
-flowering *Crocus* and *Hyacinthus*,
and the summer-flowering
Hemerocallis or day lily: also
Amaryllis, *Hippeastrum*, and *Narcissus*)

A blow struck by jealous Zephyrus, or
Boreas, by other accounts:
his skin annotated by the wound
that explicates his mortality

in red pencil, wind edits him down to
withering perennial, shriveled bulb

(perhaps a pre-Hellenic god, his
precise relationship to Apollo
still obscure, though clearly
a subordinate)

Him with a hole I keep trying
to make, dead meat of white
blooms in hand

(onion as well, garlic, leek,
chive, and asparagus)

And where he was
this leafless stalk (bluebell,
tulip, torch lily, trillium:
snowdrop, Solomon's
seal) I break to take for my own,
black at the core of blossoming

(a bell shaped nodding flower,
usually solitary)

Iconography Says:

In that year I was perfect
and in mourning

Blue glass tends to replace
lapis, I look out and it's
winter: from my window
I see only afternoons, white
silent trumpet flowers, each
abiding in its proper exile, come
to better terms, wrong air
where voice is theft itself

Tamper, tempered, sun throws me
like a shadow, very unlike a day
between two rains (and in
describing, it was that nothing
which defended me, dearest
unknown, dear why, why not
as well: presence
of thing without a thing)

Hedge, thicket, shawled
shrubs, picket of foliage, leaves
green, browning debris: yellow
trees in series, short histories
of color (four hours
of purple, four hours of red):
raw vessel of wet winds
left wordless, eventual

Wherever risk accumulates
and he unlooses all the wings,

shifts picture planes, tectonic
plates apart: petty exterminations
ruined by gone (our lord in
the tense "not yet," many
things being there, you are
elsewhere), the dangers of less

Selfish, I keep all these for me

Apollo Steps in Daphne's Footprints

Everywhere one turns
a god, someone turning into one
(cedar, cypress, sandalwood
camphor tree, cinnamon, juniper)
green as new time ripening
on the vine, hunting shoots
down into bloom, relays
and intermittencies

I made her, break her down
to twig stripped clean, a girl
-shaped slip of driftwood, mandrake
root that makes a fatal sound

She's made of some aromatic wood
(common myrtle, eucalyptus) and
I'm running after trees, tripping
over brambles, creepers and fragrant
underbrush, magnolia or japonica
(sperm smell over everything). One branch
just out of reach, sweet smelling leaves
some kindling, good for burning through
October to the season's
other side, smoke for the bees

Tracking the scent of lack
through rills and branches, freshets
streaming over pebbles (scent of
no, not at all, overpowering
odor of negation), I lost the trail

(she's moving further
into verblessness, the roots
of meaning: true aloe, not
these bracts of sassafras
and cassia: bees swathe
her in hum, leave the honey
behind, beetles pollinate her)

and ran into a tree (I am
the hunted?), stayed there
centuries (fox to the wolves
that tear summer in half?)
a light seen through
dense crowns: *Laurus nobilis*
sweet bay, bay laurel, noon's
lush lingua, sexual lexicon

A pocketful of fame in the hand
crushed leaves staining the air
I place this chaplet on my brow
(a crown of wintergreen)
and I am the sun

A Little Bitter Commentary

Autumn draws on the head
of a pin, hammered wall
of overcast, forecast
-ing gray: aging wind
shudder unrudders open
shutter's stuttering plague
of butterflies, outer
day's cast off shell
casing. Subtracted
from itself, the hell of sex
extinguished: leaves falling
sickness made sense
of rain, hail, names
hide in no one.

Sheer reason buys
the past, blunt penny
buried in hydrangea
soil: iron filings, alum
turn March acid blue. Cures,
too, have been taken
in salt flats still drunk
with the Cretaceous, cetacean
wealth of blubber, lamp wick
oil: essential ambergris
infuses what you get
is less than seen, more
than sea (absent now
from any case).

Shattered green (scattered)
grass or glass from this

distance, in love, or thought of
as: a stain on the real, just
sum of added damages,
the speaking leaf or rot
tacking boys' summer to
gone. Word boy, water
strider, carrying the tenor, hero
vehicle, another key
to all mythologies. Before one
there must be two, between
them merely difference: a can't
-claim-this-for-mind, a *the*.

Wicker Man Marginalia

For Lawrence White

madrona taken for magnolia
sperm-scented old world
blossoming: when they saw the terraces
of white tepals, they named it
Magnolia Hill, seminal
bluff overcoming new water

&

words break me, break
from me, branchlets
glinting gray in moon
-light, slivered green by day

&

Arbutus menziessi, laurelwood
trees correspond to trees
(evergreen magnolia, bull
bay, laurel bay: *Magnolia
grandiflora*, laurel magnolia)

&

the bud bursts, naked genitalia
of the swollen-open tree,
the immaculate bruise flowers
and unfolds, everything
is alive but me, my words
mere wounds

&

and the long leaves wave in an
ocean's afternoon, an air

of drowning, traffic in
distractions, depictions, describe

❧

I touch the break in history
and it stains my hand, hard
surfaced leather-textured broadleaf
coated in inflammable wax, burns
fiercely even when green

Ich komme, Grünende Brüder

❧

leaf charred by October
red shift, controlled burn trying
to build a little distance, heat
to ochre history, sienna, umber
brush fires flood dry hills

❧

wood resembles wood
the wind hauls in my voice
like catch, and I direct the plunder

Lighthouse Wreckage

Tanker run aground on shoals of disbelief,
pieces of tanker everywhere, oil
overturned on television, filming white walls
with blue clouds, strangled cormorants. Off-white,

2

stained archipelago, glyph inked across salt
water stilled to stone, a myth of maps. A fragment

3

of the Roman lighthouse at Dover
survives, shudder of sedimentary rock
a bluff, promise unkept: limestone
and strait aren't speaking today.

Chalk uplands that form the famous
white cliffs, towers fully exposed
to open sea, delivered and drowned.

4

Rusted key washed on no strand, sea
-board, shingle to cling to, rest on (*are your feet
on the rock?* artificial, at best shipped in).
Two guys at the Belmont Rocks starting a fire
in a rusted garbage can (*beacon fires kindled
on hilltops, the earliest references*): too hot today

for ashes spiraling, sparks sailing and collapsing,
exhausted: they want to rest. (*Ranging*
in elevation from 602 feet in the west
to 246 feet in the east, the greatest drop)

Burning mainly wood, coal, torches in the open,
though oil lamps and candles were also used.

5

Initially these structures
were made of wood, but wooden towers
often washed away in severe storms.
(*And their 1,160 miles*
of accompanying waterways.)

6

Large dead fish dusted with dirty sand
(a second set of scales, no use
to it at all) beside the lake, intact, but
siphoned out, the life. Eyes and part of
the tail hollowed out, just as her poem
promised: *sea bass*, it said, where there is
no sea. Something almost asking to be of use,
the smell sharp, sudden, but missing something.

7

From the sea a lighthouse may be identified
by the shape or color of its
structure, color or flash pattern
of its light.

8

Except from December to April, when
the artery is blocked by ice: time passes
down a rope knotting a swamped barge to
a rotting pier (piers always rotting in
such poems, ropes frayed: drowned quays
at North Avenue Beach, low clouds
filigreed by reflective poisons and a glint
of sun), too slowly to be measured out
in fathoms, soundings, plumb lines,
sling the lead.

By the time the tower was completed,
the island was completely submerged
at high water.

9

Superior, Michigan, Huron, Erie,
Ontario, descending in order of size
to the Atlantic, pouring themselves
into Ocean. One's been misplaced.

(*Owing to the undermining
of the foundation rock.*)

10

[Middle English *Atlantik*, from Latin
(mare) Atlanticum, Atlantic (sea),
from Greek *(pelagos) Atlantikos*, from *Atlas*,
Atlant- : of the Titan Atlas, pertaining
or belonging to.]

11

1. Derived or coming from; originating at or from: *men of the Arctic Ocean.*
2. Caused by; resulting from: *a death of drowning.*
3. Away from; at a distance from: *a mile east of the lake.*
4. So as to be separated or relieved from: *cured of hydrocephalus.*
5. From the total or group comprising: *most of the plankton gone.*
6. Composed or made from: *a dress of watered silk.*
8. Belonging or connected to: *slats of a lifeguard's tower, several broken.*
9. b. On one's part: *unfathomable of you.*
10. Containing or carrying: *a basket of driftglass and mussels.*
11. Specified as; named or called: *at a depth of ten thousand feet.*
12. Centering on; directed toward: *a love of rockbound coasts.*
13. Produced by; issuing from: *products of the Caspian Sea.*
14. Characterized or identified by: *seven years of drought.*
15. a. With reference to; about: *will speak of currents later.*
    b. In respect to: *slow of flow.*
16. Set aside for; taken up by: *a day of rest and skimming gulls.*
19. By: *beloved of many rivers.*

Light traveling at 186,282 miles
per second, but seeming
to stand still: guiding him into
the riptide, easing toward the rocks.
Extinguished now in any case.

(*Wood fires not completely discontinued
until 1800.*)

The undertow invites, inveighs,
and down he goes the waterspout
of self, wet spider legs to conjugate
the verb *to founder*, finally found.
(*When it was swept away without a trace*
in a storm of exceptional severity.)

This gives a beam that can be seen from twenty
nautical miles in clear weather.

14

By excavation of sand, it is sunk into
the seabed to a depth of up to fifty feet,
listens there to the local storm report
in the wake of which wind wavers
(how water begins): echo far inland, drowned
man's singing sink (seven minutes
at the most), what they think water is for.

Photogram: Submerged Rocks

For Forrest Gander

The sea is a collector of bodies
beloved unfamiliar surface
nothing underneath, nothing
in my hands: sharp moods

of lush obsidian headlands
angles, shadows, lapidary
light on black skin shine
His body considered as machine

made thing with impossibility
shackled to it, winch and hinge
My reinvention of the fruit of race
fine verdant particulars

dispensed against the retina:
handfuls of fuckable gods
rubbing two thighs together
to start a fire, here's a

compensatory calla lily
making math, white flower
of an hermaphroditic phallus
Moth sound cinched to boiling

glass, noon's incandescent
bulb, a friendship of sugar and needles
designed for being burned, burning
a gate in the middle of nothing

Well ordered this ardor
sweat seams tightening
scrotum to perineum, he bares
white buttocks to the page

Justice: An Ode

There was a man in the land,
he is green before the sun, the sinews
of his stones are wrapped together,
but he shall not be gathered

The flood breaketh out from the inhabitant
skin for skin (*Am I a sea, or a whale?*)
and the teeth of the young lions are broken
which are blackish by reason of the ice

If they destroy him from his place, it shall deny
him and bind their faces in secret
on the left hand, where he doth work:
dead things are formed under the waters

But put forth thine hand now
and fill him with the east wind
No mention shall be made of coral
and the chambers of the south

Through the scent of water and the inhabitants
thereof (even the waters forgotten
of the foot), remember that my life
is wind, fenced with bones and sinews

Did I say, *Bring unto me? Pursue the dry
stubble and the arms of the fatherless
which made Arcturus, Orion, and Pleiades
enter the treasures of the snow?*

Thou hast plentifully declared the thing as
it is, and hangeth the earth upon

nothing, made a decree for the rain
and said, *There is a man child conceived*

in league with the stones of the field
where the slain are, the blackness
of day: and now I am their song
Who can open the doors of his face?

Semantics at Four P.M.

He smiles, says *What's happening?*
and I say somewhere
someone's setting electrodes to someone's testicles
who's been immersed two hours in ice water

up to his shoulders, he can't remember
what day it used to be. Somewhere someone
is being disemboweled with a
serrated blade, fish-knife

to slit open two fresh trout
he had for dinner last
week, Wednesday celebration
sizzling in its battered aluminum pan

over an open campfire
in a clearing, gleaming
pan and fish and fire and the water
that put out the fire, and

he looks down at his intestines, small
and large uncoiling, spoiling
by the unpaved road, surprised
the slick should glisten so, even

at noon, this close
to the equator, is it still summer
there, I never can remember
seasons. Several things are

happening, someone is being kicked repeatedly
in the ribs by three cops (he's black, blue

by now too, purple boot
marks, bruise treads), someone else

keeps falling against the wet cement floor
of his holding cell, he can't stop
falling, somebody
stop him, then he does, stopped watch, old

-fashioned, with a broken
spring coil mechanism, and someone
could find it facedown on the sidewalk, hold it
up to the light, say *I can fix this*,

but doesn't. Somewhere four teenaged boys
are playing hackeysack by a stream bed
on the verge of story, one
has an erection he wants

to go down, and someone thinks about
dinner, someone says *Sure looks like rain*.

Transitional Objects

Five senses lead to sense,
black fruit tethered to fact

in time of empty corridor.
Caesar's feet burn in the palace

sunken under Alexandria, Eros
undresses restlessness (quickly,

hurry into, entail): stallion
tamer, namer wind, lame

as any broken storm or artifact
of interrupted wings. Precipitate,

what's left behind, what's lees,
and reticent, what tarnishes

to copper green and blue patina,
unusable parts of grief. I gather

the limbs of Osiris (white
stone's black-body glyphs),

bramble gods ruin skin: all
ghosts created equal (statuary

bronze, more strictly a brass)
without the necessary powerlessness.

Some day I could be danger.

A man should have something
of tree, of horse, of ship billowing

about him: Apollo statue naked
for modesty's sake, with desire

scrawled down the thigh
disguised as painted marble,

sartorius, terra cotta, gaudy
bronze geometry of femur, linea

aspera, quadriceps femoris,
adductors longus, brevis, and magnus:

his shrugged-off immortality
is careful to say little. Articulate

damage half occasion, half conjectured
plaster, wasps hover above his grave:

dog rose, oleander, terebinth
(a small tree yielding turpentine).

I made that afternoon museum mine.

Occurrences across the Chromatic Scale

The way air is at the same time
intimate and out of reach

(a void with light inside it
turned on a wheel of wheres)

Stars' lease on sky expires, breathes
in leisures of sparrows, wrens

and casual trees, wet sidewalks
twittering with tattered news, old

leaves (hollow bones and branches)
wind of wish and which and boys

waiting for white kisses, rain
of feathers, clouds saving their later

Suppose this sunlight, day split open
suppose these senses and the information

carried, thing and news of the thing
repeating *place*, location of position

Birds, for example, remembered
fluttering torn terms, congregations

shimmer of hummingbirds
but when does one see more than one

tumbling bright flesh (sky
at hand) pleating afternoon, banking

on mere atmosphere, primary
colors dividing white into

three clean halves (red, green,
blue-bitter berries rasp, crabapples

crush underfoot), the spectrum
says *don't stop there*

(smudged light a lapse of attention)
there's never enough world for you

Frame

Someone's smeared a dirty rag
across daylight, some bird
just sound, then out of sound.
Worn siding, yellow brickwork,
posts and joists to puzzle out
a street, block of cobbles
on the left, bad house, good truck, bad
trees (slung willows slanting green
to yellow in the elevated train
tracks wind), bed of red leaves
on lawn. Scrap of bird, cardinal
flaw in air, at home there
as anywhere the wind leafs
through. Signs wandering, FIRST
WARD GACKLE, River
Drive, I promised myself
words, as well as weather
burnt to the touch.

Sap torn from a twig, sprig
springs back from being bent
(one closing hand, two in
the bush), but it is dead:
a thumb pressed to the wound
stems viscous flow, peels back
thick with injury, sticky
incursions of the geometric
on the organic limb, naked
economy grooved into gaze.
Doxa, reducing, reducing,
a history of color (even in rain),
single, complicit, unfinished

in retrospect. Leaf wardens, brambles
thresh and yield, I wanted
to betray him; outline filled
with fact and mimic stars
wedded a word to wood.

Cygnus

For Geoffrey Nutter

Persons reminded me of birds, a boy
who is a swan and is not mine,
white feathers that go by
clouds. He figures as constellation, clouds
in tight formation, forming him
or his impossibility of skin. That he is seen
to be beautiful, that he is called by strangers'
names, almost persuaded of September: that he
is torn from the white he makes
his home, falling as snow, down.
Boy who became a swan, buoyed through
blank night, stick figure fixed to several skies: wing
for a writing arm, he is a poet
scribbling down stars, their mouths
pinned open, hungering
in place. That he is seen to take flight
in magnitudes, that he persuades
himself to be observed at different proximities
to the horizon, that light bends
for him relative to the position he takes
regarding the sun. Star-mouth,
cloud-lip, northerly wing, my hands
are talced with a dust of feathers,
my hands are full of birds, all thumbs.
You fly through me.

IV

Littoral

One day I looked up from my imagination,
a paraphrase of freedom in the sensorium.
Little star drowned in smoke, little ghost
fuming to ash and burnt grass. The genius
of the camera absorbs him, halts reflective paper
skin, pages of meditative hair: the shutter's
gleaming eden islands light. I could enter
the surplus of it, make use of
spilled exchange: substitution
hunted down by the unique. History
is a body, "the unbearable deeds
of the blessed gods": snow under the skin,
the scorched edges of the possible
(the cold beneath the burn of it).

Delay dangles Polaris from a rusty nail,
the familiar voyage to Naxos
aborted, repeated: Arion, or another
amateur, in love with curve and wave,
god music playing underwater. (The paper
boat beached, reverting to newsprints
of the gone world, slurry
of things the voice shores up.) Summer
opens its ocean miles away, luck
drowns in its labyrinth, and somewhere
something approaching an image unfurls:
white pinpoint eyes of grackles,
the iridescent blue-black Negroes.
Despite which falls

Interglacial

White of extinct gods' etch and simmer
spills from salt heaven, pluvial
law of breakage suffering
away from himself, throat kissed
shale black. (Shall I compare thee,
incommensurate, and greet you as
a god, good substitute? Lie
still and let me listen to your skin.)
Hieratic wrack having attained
the age of representation, refutation:
see him so water, so clearly dissolved.

He wonders if he might be the visible,
spontaneous prosody of gesture,
recurrent, irretrievable, and only in part
a god, part of a god: belief fragment
worn smooth by glaciers in retreat,
abraded by the Pleistocene to glimmer,
shine, scuttle and glyph luster. Odor
of artifice, odor of lies
down in the teeming interior sea,
salt flats of Lake Bonneville
where water was slept away.

Weather Comes from the West

He's all states and princes, colonies
and continental drift, waging
plate tectonics on his way to rain:
territories of avowal and random

vowels. Clouds are interruptions
in the blue, occlusions pregnant
with rain or other inclemencies,
unkind transitions filled

with gods (my enemy muse).
Also this is the sea. Someone
looked in on color and found it lacking
something green: all treason,

heretic to froth and spume, and
the ones who stayed with nothing
inside. Night is a wire hung with
small sounds, philosophy of wolves

in eclipse, or any disposition
towards blackened white.
Sibling forest, brother
town: tides in the air, tides in

the earth, miles of lines downed
and by unlikely conditions diagnosed.

One of Their Gods

Was he lightning poured from a smashed flute,
music carved from someone's bones
I know? Qualities absently enter his mouth
where spring and snow are the same, song
-bred, sound-led: frozen in parenthesis.

Warped windows ripple like light
snow (grayed pane a single plane
waves past, wet leaves meander
winter winds), the curtness of his lyric
body, male odalisque with unlit

cigarette: in danger all the time, in winter
falling ice, in summer falling safety
glass, blue-smoke-flowering stars
uncounted as of yet, some illion or another
night obscured by streetlights, head

-lights, an oceanic black with islands
in it, incursions of opaque color
at patterned intervals, contingencies
of trees and buildings blinking out. Club
-headed weeds, wet pebbles, my beloved

is white and muddy: these tattered
bodies sheeted in news as if it were
sleep rub off on the hands,
flowerboats spilled of all cargo.
He will scatter on black waters.

Manifest

Sir star, Herr Lenz, white season body
master snapping masts in half, absent
winds' workmanship: what window
will I look you through, what brook, stream

creaking past fretwork weeds, clouds
in the context of cold? Lord knot
to be untied, skiff hard alee ill winds:
a hiss of wish and cinders and I

am warm, crossing dazed oceans by hand
to sow the doubtful sea with drought. Mine
of rain and seize and sluice, you change

your mind again, a rage for green waves'
open vowels, undrinkable. No talking
to the weeds, no talking with the snow.

Unravel

The other, then, is the one
one outlives, uncertain gathering
around an emptiness:

the river deepening
into doubt, drought
of cottonwoods on either side

Bees sow the toil of lilies
reproducing fields and empty
lots, reap the pollen boiling
into honey, sunlight seeping
through the fingers, skin
and hair: tangle of sticky
daylight clings to lips and tongue

(So much remains to be seen
in other men's seasons, five
and ten night stands
of sugar maple, alder, birch)

Wet sidewalk blares *Now*
and the days heat up, October
dissimulation, Indian
giver (orange, melon, cerise,
a kiss of seven pomegranate
seeds to catch summer's fall,
stammer of nodding poppies)

This time of year (air
stamped with static, alley
of thrum and drone)
they're everywhere

The Practice of Goodbye

The young sing *es eiona*
while the old men laugh and clap
in the direction of suspicion:

these dour suburban bacchants
(perennials grown as annuals)
killing the lions and harmless wasps

Purple ornamental kale in corner
pots, planters of silver-furred dusty miller
make a boundary, flower late or not at all:

semen tints the atmosphere,
landscape oblique to occasion
hammering summer boys to heat

Paint and ruined blossoms,
melancholic white men
scattered with torn petals, tanagers

disaster, lovely saunter
down damp streets, were the gods
ever so in love with their own lies

My horizon will be pounding waves
of horses, white breaking
across black rocks at bay

light flooding water, promise
or threat: anywhere risk
accumulates, the hands wash ashore

The muddled windows (melting),
the ripped desiccated branch (awaiting
which) maintain the wind:

death-dealing Eros
extinguishes the torch
and I am disappearance

Imaginary Elegy

The manifest scatters likeness
like white light, gods
cut through my body like a sword
in the hands of a dead hero, he who
accomplishes, whittles
me down into perfection, or if
I won't, then less than that,
an absence at the edges
of narration, mention me. Love
burns like incense in gold censers
and cannot forgive (empire
of essential oils annexing air),
who can withstand
being loved for long.

When light pours out of me
(like love, resembling, resembling),
citronella oil and myrrh, white
peppermint, less hardy
and more prized, like blood
whose savor is sweet
in the nostrils of gods
when it steams on
uncovered altars, streams from
the fresh-cut throat. I would
be beautiful, burnt wilderness
at bay, and what would that
be like? Siege of light glints, nicks
marred skin. Elektra always forgets

Iphigeneia, bitch sister
sharpening the blades, the finest silver.

The Anania Butterfly

For Michael Anania

. . . and then the gold recedes, composition
retreats to black and white: *Anania*
funebris (so signed by Ström, 1768), resembling

a yellow jacket having put on mourning
dress, prepared for a more formal
diurn. A dusting of minute scales

embarrasses each wing with four lakes
of talcum, lime, chalk, salt:
unswimmable in any case. Body

a branch of light burned down
to charcoal striped with symmetrical
ash, the past of the imago must be

imagined. Pyraloidea, Pyralidae, Pyraustinae,
Anania, oblique descents into
the specified, the labor of the senses

laying down tundra from Scandinavia
to Siberia: Lepidoptera, "scaly wing,"
Linnaeus loves the names of things. This

color photograph from the Altai
Mountains, where half-light's remembered
and world is wed to word.

Notes

"Kingdom: An Epithalamium" is composed entirely of phrases from the Song of Solomon in the King James Version and from the notes to that book in *The Oxford Annotated Bible*. They have been condensed and reordered, but only four pronouns have been changed.

"Wing Under Construction": Ophiussa, Alasiya, Yadnana, Kipros, and Kubris are ancient names in various languages for Cyprus, famed for its extensive copper deposits. The island's pre-Hellenic people and culture had strong links with both Phoenicia and Minoan Crete.

"In the City of Elagabal" is primarily composed of phrases from the King James Version of the Bible, Joseph Campbell's *The Masks of God: Occidental Mythology*, Edward Gibbons's *The Decline and Fall of the Roman Empire*, Gerhard Herm's *The Phoenicians: The Purple Empire of the Ancient World*, Serge Lancel's *Carthage: A History*, Fergus Millar's *The Roman Near East: 31 BC to AD 337*, W. W. Tarn's *Hellenistic Civilisation*, and Robert Turcan's *The Cults of the Roman Empire*. I have been extremely free in my treatment of these sources.

"Fire sacrifices in which animals or even men are burned wholly, holocausts, are characteristic of the religion of the West Semites, the Jews, and Phoenicians. Children were still burned in Carthage in historical times, and in Jerusalem the daily burning of two one-year-old lambs in the temple became the center of the divine service" (Walter Burkert, *Greek Religion*). In Mediterranean countries summer is the barren season: the burning sun is the enemy. The collocation of sacrificial child immolation (practiced not only in Carthage and Phoenicia but by the ancient Israelites), cyclical myths of the dying and reborn vegetation god, and Near Eastern and Imperial Roman solar cults is my own.

"Roman Year": The Roman year originally consisted of ten lunar months, and began in March (*Martius*). The months January (*Januarius*) and February (*Februarius*) were added to the calendar by King Numa Pompilius to close a previously uncounted winter gap of fifty days between December and March. The months we now know as July (*Julius*) and August (*Augustus*) originally had the names *Quintilis* and *Sextilis*, respectively, the fifth and sixth months of the year.

"Hygiene": The quote in section two is from an interview with the novelist Dennis Cooper in the men's fashion magazine *Details*. Psychoanalyst Jacques Lacan points out that madness is an exercise of the most rigorous logic. For example, if you love someone, you want to incorporate and become one with him. Jeffrey Dahmer literalized this impulse.

"Wicker Man Marginalia": *"Ich komme, Grünende Brüder"* is from the transformation scene of Strauss's opera *Daphne*, in which Daphne becomes a laurel tree. It means "I come, green brothers," her greeting to the beloved trees whose ranks she is joining.

"Photogram: Submerged Rocks": A photogram is an image made by placing objects on a piece of photographic paper and exposing the composition to light; we made them in fifth grade with amethysts and washers. Man Ray, the major modern practitioner of the form, modestly called his photograms "rayographs."

"Justice: An Ode" is composed entirely of phrases from the Book of Job in the King James Version. They have been condensed and reordered, but only one pronoun has been changed.

"Imaginary Elegy": Much of the language and imagery of this poem is inspired by the final scene of Richard Strauss's opera *Elektra*, libretto by Hugo von Hofmannsthal, based on his adaptation of Sophocles's play (mediation is all!). The single-minded drive to avenge the father represses Klytemnestra's *motivation* for killing Agamemnon: he killed their daughter Iphigeneia (Elektra's sister), summoned to Aulis by a ruse and sacrificed for the sake of a favorable wind. The poem takes its title from Jack Spicer's "Imaginary Elegies," though he wrote five more than I have managed.

Many of the poems in this volume were inspired by Roberto Calasso's brilliant and wayward meditation on classical myth, *The Marriage of Cadmus and Harmony*. I owe an enormous debt to the *Encyclopedia Britannica* CD-ROM (1996), which has been a great source of information and even phrasing, particularly with regard to botanical materials.

Acknowledgments

The poems in this book (sometimes in earlier versions) have appeared in the following journals, to whose editors grateful acknowledgment is made: *Agni* ("Manifest"); *American Letters and Commentary* ("Semantics at Four P.M."); *The American Poetry Review* ("Burnt from the Notebooks," "Iconography Says:"); *The Bellingham Review* ("Photogram: Submerged Rocks"); *Boston Book Review* ("Blue One Lake"); *The Boston Review* ("Syntax"); *Chelsea* ("The Anania Butterfly"); *Chicago Review* ("Kingdom: An Epithalamium"); *Colorado Review* ("Imaginary Elegy"); *Conjunctions* ("Flicker," "Justice: An Ode," "The Practice of Goodbye," "Roman Year"); *Denver Quarterly* ("Confluence," "A Little Bitter Commentary," "Unravel"); *Fence* ("Three Songs about Snow"); *Indiana Review* ("An Abbreviated History of Signs"); *The Iowa Review* ("Cygnus"); *The Journal* ("Weather Comes from the West"); *New England Review* ("The Invention of Longitude"); *Notre Dame Review* ("Polaroid"); *The Paris Review* ("Reasons for Living"); *Partisan Review* ("Interglacial"); *Ploughshares* ("Apollo on What the Boy Gave"); *Poetry New York* ("Wing Under Construction"); *Seneca Review* ("*Amant Marine*," "Frame," "Transitional Objects"); *TriQuarterly* ("Apollo Steps in Daphne's Footprints"); *Verse* ("Homology," "Occurrences across the Chromatic Scale," "One of Their Gods," "Les Semblables"); *The Virginia Quarterly Review* ("Littoral"); and *Volt* ("Wicker Man Marginalia").

"In the City of Elagabal," "Lighthouse Wreckage," "Little Hands," and "Periplus" appeared in my chapbook *Periplus of the Previous Life*, part of the *Black Warrior Review* chapbook series.

An early version of "Hygiene" appeared in *Chicago Review*; a revised version appeared in *Callaloo*. The original version also appeared in *Real Things: An Anthology of Popular Culture in American Poetry*, edited by Jim Elledge and Susan Swartwout and published by Indiana University Press.

"Semantics at Four P.M." also appeared in *The Best American Poetry 2000*, guest edited by Rita Dove and published by Scribner.

"Little Hands," "Semantics at Four P.M.," and "Les Semblables" also appeared in *Word of Mouth: An Anthology of Gay American Poetry*, edited by Timothy Liu and published by Talisman House.

"Interglacial" also appeared in *Passing the Word: Writers on Their Mentors*, edited by Jeffrey Skinner and Lee Martin and published by Sarabande Books.

"Little Hands" appeared on-line at *Web Conjunctions*.

I'd like to thank Chris Cutrone, Jocelyn Emerson, Catherine Imbriglio, Jenny Mueller, and most especially Lawrence White (poetic interlocutor nonpareil) for their comments, encouragement, and inspiration. I'd also like to thank two lost friends, Amy England and Megan Orr, for their poetic companionship during the writing of many of these poems. With this, my fourth book, it may be time to acknowledge some of my former teachers; in their various ways they contributed to the making of the poet that I am today. Among them I would like to single out Ben Belitt, Alvin Feinman, Jorie Graham, Philip Levine, Heather McHugh, and Michael Anania. I am also grateful to the Illinois Arts Council for a poetry fellowship and to the Howard Foundation for a Merit Award, both of which helped me to complete this volume.

Reginald Shepherd was born in New York City in 1963 and raised in tenements and housing projects in the Bronx. He received his B.A. from Bennington College in 1988 and M.F.A. degrees from Brown University (1991) and the University of Iowa (1993). The University of Pittsburgh Press published his first book, *Some Are Drowning*, in 1994 as winner of the 1993 AWP Award Series in Poetry. Pittsburgh published his second book, *Angel, Interrupted*, in 1996; it was a finalist for a 1997 Lambda Literary Award. His chapbook *This History of His Body* was published by Thorngate Road in 1998. His third collection, *Wrong*, was published by the University of Pittsburgh Press in 1999.

Shepherd is the recipient of a 1993 "Discovery" / *The Nation* Award, a 1993 Paumanok Poetry Award, the 1994–1995 Amy Lowell Poetry Travelling Scholarship, the 1994 George Kent Prize from *Poetry*, a 1995 NEA creative writing fellowship, a 1998 Illinois Arts Council poetry fellowship, and a 2000 Saltonstall Foundation poetry grant. His poems have appeared in *The American Poetry Review, Conjunctions, The Gettysburg Review, The Iowa Review, The Kenyon Review, The Nation, The New York Times Book Review, The Paris Review, Partisan Review, Ploughshares, Poetry, TriQuarterly*, and *The Yale Review*, as well as in the 1995, 1996, 2000, and 2002 editions of *The Best American Poetry*.